Rhymes and Riddles to Rattle Your Reason!

ILLUSTRATED BY VERITY RICHARDS

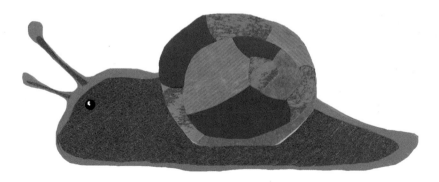

MARION BOYARS
CHILDREN'S

These riddles are harder than they look, are you ready?

"I am! I am! Try us!"

I'm called by a man's name
though I'm small as a mouse.
When winter comes I love to be
with my red target near the house.

Answer: *a robin*

At night they come
without being fetched
and by day they are lost
without being stolen.

Answer: *the stars*

My sides are firmly laced about
yet nothing is within.
You'll think my head is strange indeed
being nothing else but skin.

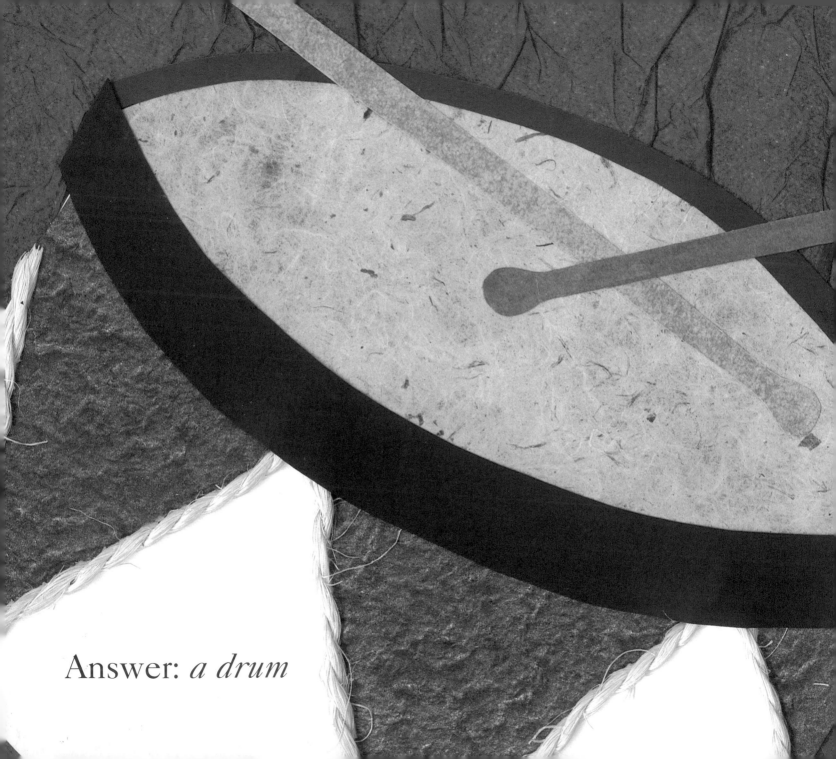

Answer: *a drum*

If a man carried my burden
he would break his back.
I am not rich
but leave silver in my track.

*This is a tricky one
so think carefully...*

Answer: *a snail*

Each morning I appear
to lie at your feet.
All day I will follow
no matter how fast you run,
yet I nearly perish
in the midday sun.

Answer:
your shadow

When I am filled
I can point the way.
When I am empty
nothing moves me.
I have two skins
one without and one within.

Answer: *a glove*

In spring I look gay
decked in handsome array,
in summer more clothing I wear.
When colder it grows
I fling off my clothes,
and in winter quite naked appear.

Here's a clue to help you:
birds like building nests in these!

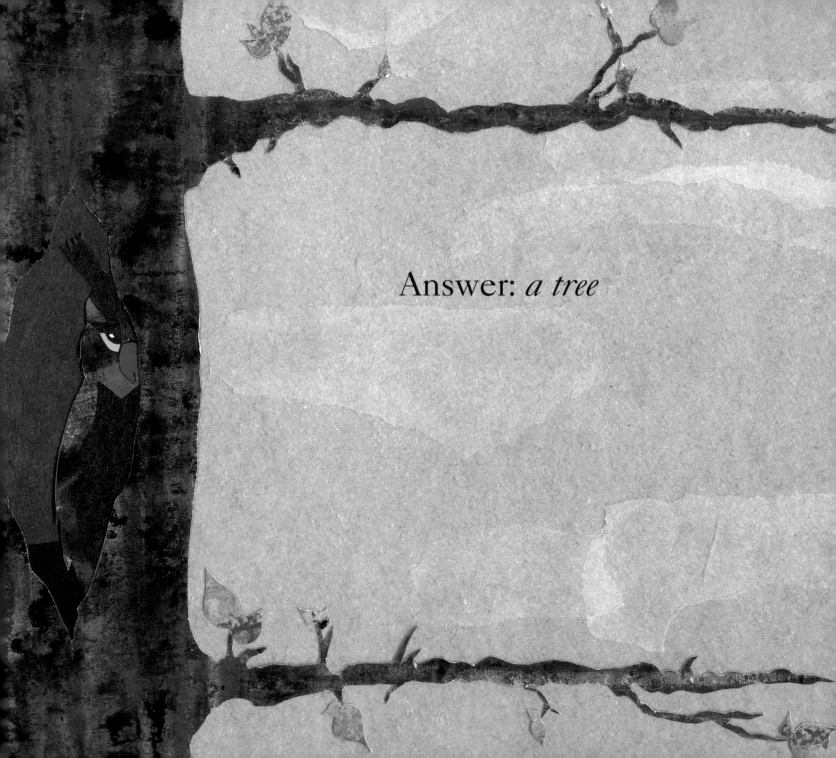

Answer: *a tree*

My father is the sun-god,
my mother is the sea,
my house is in the heavens,
the moonbeams play with me.

My gown has seven colours,
my song has seven keys,
I run among the mountains,
I bathe within the seas.

The world is ever waiting
for the tinkling little cry
of the bangles on my ankles
as I leap across the sky.

What am I?

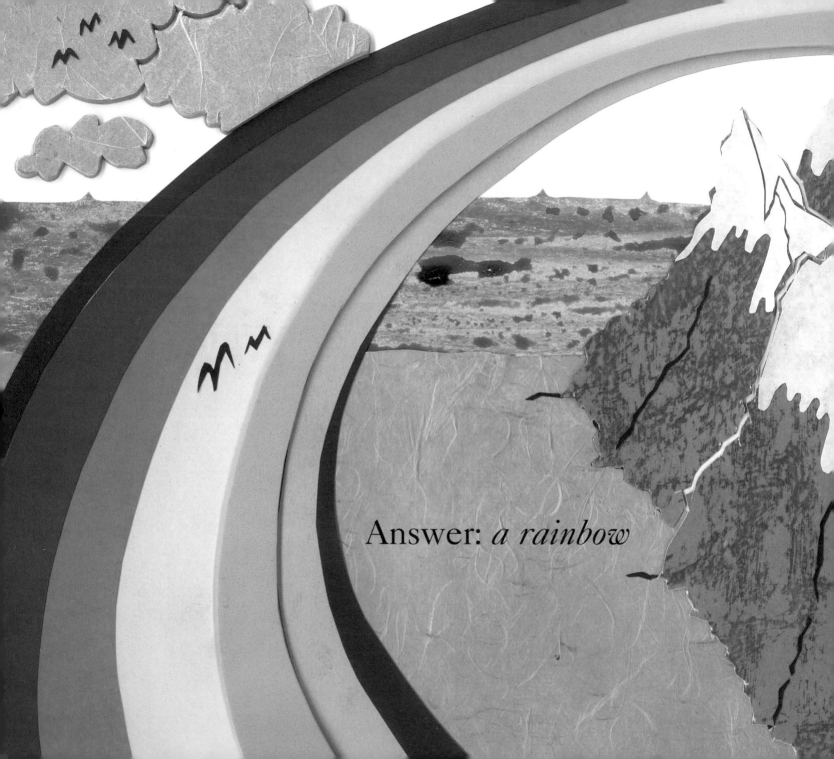

Answer: *a rainbow*

As round as an apple,
as deep as a pail,
I will never cry out
til I'm caught by the tail.

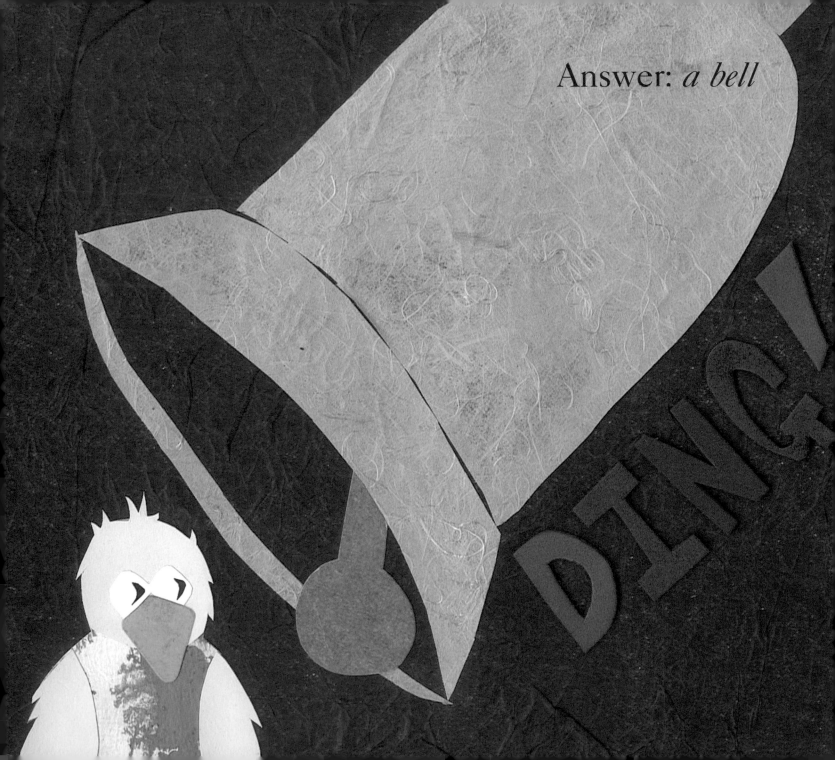

Answer: *a bell*

DING!

You heard me before
yet you'll hear me again.
Then I die
til you call me again.

Answer: *an echo*

Glittering points
that downwards thrust.
Sparkling spears
that never rust.

"Hmm... Hmm...
I know! Ask me!"

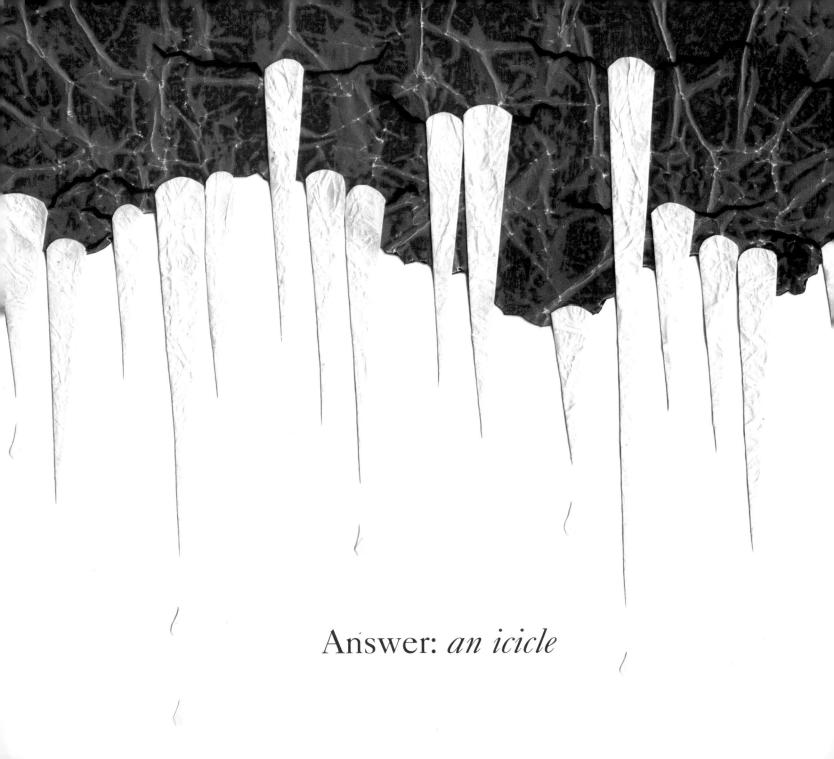

Answer: *an icicle*

I have a little house in which I live all alone. It has no doors or windows and if I want to go out I must break through the wall.

What am I?

Answer: *a chick in an egg*

Bright as diamonds,
loud as thunder,
never still,
a thing of wonder.

Answer:
a waterfall

Well done, you've worked your brains hard!
Just one more before you go, are you ready?

"Yes! Yes! We love riddles!"

I view the world in a little space
and I'm always changing place.
No food I eat but by my power
I help grow what millions devour.

Answer: *the sun*